Praying with Mary

Juliette Levivier

Illustrations by Anne Gravier

CTS Children's Books

Table of Contents

Mary, specially loved by God

And the Virgin's name was Mary.

Luke 3:4

It was not by chance that Anne and Joachim called their daughter Mary. For the Jews, a person's name is very important. It says something about that person. The Hebrew name Myriam (Mary in English) is often used in the Bible. It can have as many as fifty different meanings!

In Aramaic, the language that Jesus spoke, it meant "Sovereign Lady" or "Lady", like when we call her "Our Lady". In Egyptian it meant "Loved by God". How beautiful! Mary really is God's beloved!

I love to use this sweet name as a prayer, with the greatest reverence.

Maria

Mary, chosen before time began,

Angels and saints love you, and God loves
you most of all.

Royal Queen of Heaven and of mankind,

Your love and watchful tenderness fill our
hearts and our lives.

5

Mary's names

*May the name of Mary be always on your lips,
always in your hearts.*

St Bernard

When you have said "Mary", you've said everything. All love, all joy, all beauty, all greatness – absolutely everything! But from earliest times Christians have given their Heavenly Mother lots of other loving names, just like when we say "Mummy darling" to our own mother. All of these names put together make up "litanies". These are very ancient prayers that express all our reverence for Mary.

Some of these names are a bit mysterious and sometimes surprising. Each of them says something about Mary. They are like precious stones set in the crown of Mary, our Queen.

How beautiful these names for Mary are! I can sing them softly or recite them. They make up the most beautiful prayers.

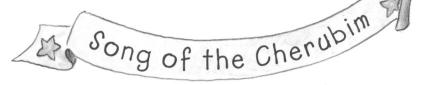

Song of the Cherubim

How lovely all your names are, Mary!
Full of reverence and poetry,
they sing your glory.
Refuge of sinners, Tower of ivory,
City of God, Gate of Heaven,

Canticle of the Seraphim

House of gold, Spiritual vessel,   7
Health of the sick, Mirror of justice,
Star, rose, lily.

As we sing these litanies
we contemplate the marvels
that God has worked in you.

Joy of the Archangels

Immaculate Mary

You are all fair, my beloved,
there is no flaw in you.

Song of Songs 4:7

"I am the Immaculate Conception." That's a difficult word! Bernadette wondered what it meant. She ran straight to the parish priest at Lourdes to tell him about these strange words. He understood them perfectly: the beautiful lady who appeared to Bernadette in a grotto was the Blessed Virgin Mary!

"Immaculate" means "without stain". From the very first moment of her life, Mary was preserved from the stain of original sin. She was conceived without sin to carry the Son of God made man in her womb. She is immaculate for Jesus, whom she is to carry within herself, and through Jesus, who preserved her from all sin.

Mary is so beautiful! I contemplate her in silence.

O Mary, you never committed any sin.
Keep my heart from evil.
Give me the strength to do good.
I really want to be like you, Mary!
Transform me, purify me.

Give me a pure heart,
a transparent heart to receive Jesus.

O Mary, you are so beautiful,
you are Immaculate!

Mary,
full of grace

Hail, full of grace,
the Lord is with you.

Luke 1:28

What a strange greeting for a young girl! Mary must have been really surprised. It is because the Lord is with her, because the Holy Spirit dwells in her heart, that Mary is "full of grace" – everything in her is love.

She is "filled with grace" like a golden vessel filled to the brim with precious perfume.

She is "full" because she is so close to God that she lives on his joy: all her happiness is in him.

The grace that she is "filled with, filled full and overflowing", as Saint Bernard said, she doesn't keep for herself. She gives it to us without reserve.

Through Mary, I am filled with God's grace. I receive everything from God through her.

Upon all of us, O Mary,
you pour out the streams of your grace
like a fountain of pure water.
You flood us with your blessings.
The torrent of love
that springs from the heart of Jesus
is given to us through you.

Thank you, Jesus, for this life-giving water.
Thank you, Jesus, for Mary.

11

Mary,
radiance of joy

*My soul magnifies the Lord
and my spirit rejoices in God my Saviour.*

Luke 1:46-47

How joyful the angels are! Of course – because they bring us God's own joy.

On that day the Angel Gabriel was full of joy. He was going to announce to Mary that she had been chosen to be the mother of the Saviour whom the world had been awaiting for so long. What wonderful news!

When Mary said yes, she shared the angel's joy, and her joy spread to the whole universe: joy for everyone, because Jesus was coming into the world for every single one of them.

Mary invites me to rejoice with her over this incredible news: Jesus is coming to set me free from death and sin! Alleluia!

Μy soul magnifies the Lord
and my spirit rejoices in God my Saviour.
He has looked on the lowliness of
his handmaiden.
From now on,
all generations will call me blessed.
He who is mighty
has done great things for me,
Holy is his Name.

Luke 1:46-48

13

Mary's Yes

Let it be done to me according to your word!

Luke 1:38

Mary was a very young girl. She lived in Nazareth, a little village in Galilee, with her parents, her family, friends and neighbours. Throughout her childhood Mary lived a simple, happy life, marked by the rhythm of prayer and listening to the word of God. In her there was no refusal, no wickedness, no lying.

So when the angel announced to her that God had chosen her to be the mother of the Saviour, she may have been surprised, but she was ready. Ready to say yes to God. This yes at the Annunciation was not her first yes, nor her last. But it was the one that gave us Jesus our Saviour. She would have to say yes many more times in order to follow Jesus right to the end!

Mary teaches me to say yes to God. She helps me to turn towards her Son every day of my life.

Holy Virgin Mary
every day you had
to find your way
of saying yes to God.
Every day you had
to start discovering God
in your life again
in a completely different way
from the one you expected.
Teach us not to be
a page that's already written on,
but a clean page
every day
where the Spirit of God can
write the marvels he works in us.

(from a prayer by
Cardinal Roger Etchegaray)

Mary, filled with
the Holy Spirit

*Blessed are you among women
and blessed is the fruit of your womb!*

Luke 1:42

Quick, quick, no time to lose! Mary put some things together, said goodbye to her friends and set off for the house of her cousin Elizabeth, who was also expecting a baby. Mary hadn't known before about the birth of Jesus, or thought about making a long journey to help her cousin Elizabeth. But she allowed herself to be led by the Holy Spirit, ready for whatever he asked of her. Jesus, whom she carried within her womb, led her to other people. Mary teaches us to let ourselves be turned around, to let ourselves be led by the Spirit.

God never stops surprising me! He's there where he's least expected, always loving, always concerned for our happiness. And what if he upsets all my ideas and plans? So much the better!

God has blessed you, O Mary.
Out of all women, he has chosen you.
In you the Messiah is growing.
You are the dwelling-place of the Spirit.

You run through the hills
to reach your cousin Elizabeth and share
your joy with her.
Thank you, Mary,
for bringing me your Son Jesus.
I find all my joy in him.

17

Mary,
mother of Jesus

She gave birth to her first-born son, and wrapped him in swaddling-clothes and laid him in a manger.

Luke 2:7

In a stable at Bethlehem, on a clear, starry night, Mary gave birth to Jesus. How much she loved her little son already! God wanted his beloved Son to have a mother, to give him life, to bring him up, to love him, and lull him to sleep, and caress him.

Softly, tenderly, she called him by his name, "Jesus", which means "God saves". Deep in her heart she knew that this tiny baby was the Saviour of the world. How would he do it? She didn't know. But what she knew was that God's love is stronger than sin and death. Jesus had come to offer that love to every single person.

Jesus lies there in Mary's arms. She holds him out to me, she gives him to me.

Lord, you have given me
such a lovely mother!
She watches over me,
she gives me all her tenderness.
She loves me so much,
and I love her so much!
I bless you for my mother!
You've also given me a mother in Heaven.
She loves me too, and watches over me.
I bless you for the Virgin Mary!

19

Holy Mary

God is everywhere, but it is in Mary
that we find him closest to us.

St Louis-Marie Grignion de Montfort

Like all mothers, Mary looked after her family. She cooked, sewed, washed the clothes, and prayed... She didn't seem to do anything special, but filled everything she did with love. That's holiness.

Mary is the greatest of all women, the holiest of all the saints. Do you know why? Because by her perfect obedience, her unshakeable faith, her unfailing love, she is specially united to God's own holiness. She is the most perfect reflection of God on earth.

Goodness, I'm not perfect at all! But I am called to be a saint. Who better than Mary can help me to become one?

You're so great, Mary,
and yet you're still so humble.
You're so powerful,
and yet you're still so gentle.
You're so perfect,
and yet you're still so modest.
O Mary, teach me to imitate you.
Lead me along the paths of holiness
so that, always and everywhere,
even in the smallest things in my life,
I can give glory to God.

Mary, mediator

They have no wine.

John 2:3

That day, Mary and Jesus were invited to a wedding at Cana. Suddenly – oh dear! There was no more wine left! The wedding-feast was going to be spoilt.

Then Mary interceded with Jesus. He changed water into wine, and joy returned!

Our attentive Mother Mary notices everything we need. She presents our prayer to our Lord. She "intercedes" for us. She doesn't answer our prayers herself: she asks Jesus, and he gives her everything. He can't refuse her anything! Through Mary, Jesus fills us with graces. Why "through Mary"? Because that's what God has decided!

Mary brings me everything that the Lord wants to give me. She's like a golden thread connecting me with Heaven.

O Mary,
I come before you to entrust to you
my joys and my sorrows,
my efforts and my failures,
what I do well,
and what I do badly.

Mary,
full of tenderness and compassion,
ask your Son Jesus
to pour out on me
his love and his forgiveness.

23

Mary's faith

Blessed is she who believed that
the Lord's promise to her would be fulfilled.

Luke 1:45

When the Angel Gabriel appeared to her, Mary believed what he told her. She believed that through her, God was going to work wonders.

At Cana, Mary believed that Jesus could turn water into wine. At the foot of the Cross, Mary stood upright. Upright, because her faith did not collapse. Later, alone in front of Jesus' tomb, she continued to believe that it wasn't all over, that Jesus would save mankind as he promised. She knew that he always kept his promises.

Mary is "she who believes", even when there seems to be no way out and no hope. She is the model of our faith.

Do I believe too that God can work wonders in my life?

With you, Mary, I want to believe.
With you, I want to hope.
With you, I want to sing.
With you, I want to praise God.
With you, I want to trust.
You lead me in the darkness.
You light up the path before my feet.
With you, Mary, I will go to Heaven.

Mary in suffering

And a sword will pierce through your own soul also.

Luke 2:35

Every time people mocked Jesus, accused him, or ill-treated him, Mary suffered too. How often was her heart pierced through? Like all mothers, she suffered with her child. She was so closely united to Jesus that she shared completely in all his sufferings, including the Cross.

She accepted Jesus' sacrifice for us. In the middle of difficulties, in spite of her sorrow, she was still full of love, faith and hope.

Mary has suffered so much herself that she understands every single one of my sufferings, every one of my sorrows. She encourages me to keep trusting God, even in my trials.

Mary, you sing when I sing.
You smile when I smile.
When I cry, you comfort me.
When I suffer, you reassure me.
Mary, you share everything
that makes up my life.
Mary, carry me when I grow weak.

27

Mary at the foot of the Cross

Standing by the cross of Jesus was his mother.

John 19:25

When everyone else had abandoned Jesus, Mary climbed to the top of Calvary. She was there when Jesus was crucified. She stood close to him, without growing weak. We don't know what she felt, but we can be sure that she was praying with all her strength, and with all her faith. That's what made her able to stand there to the end.

28

More than thirty years earlier, the Angel Gabriel announced to her that her Son Jesus would be the Saviour of mankind. And now look where men's sins had brought him!

But Mary knew how strong God's love is. She knew that he would have the last word.

United to Jesus on the Cross, she too begs God for forgiveness for all mankind.

Mary, you believed in spite of everything.
To fear, you respond with trust,
to hatred, you respond with love,
to violence, you respond with gentleness,
to opposition, you respond
with faithfulness.

Give us, O Mary,
the gift of learning,
to be faithful in trials.
Give your courage and your hope
to all those who feel weak
in the face of suffering.

Mary, mother
of mankind

Jesus said to his mother, "Woman, behold your son!"
Then he said to the disciple, "Behold your mother!"
And from that hour the disciple took her
to his own home.

John 19:26

As he died, Jesus entrusted his beloved mother to his dearest friend. In actual fact it was more that he was entrusting John to Mary. And in John every person was entrusted to Mary, for her to bring each of us to Jesus.

Like all mothers, Mary watches over us with unlimited tenderness, with love that nothing can discourage. Her maternal presence is given to us as an immense gift.

Jesus invites us to take Mary "into our own home", to live with her at every moment, to let ourselves be educated and purified by her presence.

My joys and my sorrows, my hopes and my fears, I entrust them all to Mary: she's there at the heart of my life.

You know all our joys, O Mary,
and all our sufferings and sorrows too.
All our sins, all our refusals,
and all our doubts,
you understand them all.
All your children gather under
your mantle,
they take refuge there, filled with trust.
You gather them tenderly to yourself.
Thank you, O Mary,
for consenting to be our Mother.

Mary, mother
of the Church

*All these with one accord devoted themselves to
prayer, together with the women and
Mary the mother of Jesus.*

Acts 1:14

How lucky the Apostles and the first Christians were, to
have Mary with them! She helped them to stay faithful to
Jesus' message.

Today Mary is always present with all the Christians who
make up the Church. She helps us to stay faithful to the
Gospel, she watches over us and carries us by her prayer.
Just as the sea is made up of very many drops of water, so
the Church is made up of the many people who, in Heaven,
in Purgatory, and on earth, are united to Jesus.

It's not possible to love Jesus without loving his Church.
That is why Mary, the mother of Jesus, is also the mother
of the Church.

In the Church everyone has a place, everyone is important.
By my Baptism, I belong to the Church of Christ. She needs
me too.

You are there, Mary,
close to us, in the Church:
when your children are gathered together,
in my room when I pray,
in prisons, close to those who are
persecuted because of their faith,
and in the hospitals, close to the sick.
You are there, Mary,
close to those who are dying,
close to those who
are crying,
close to those who
are laughing.
You are there where
the Church is,
where people
are praying,
where people
are singing,
where people
are living.

Mary, gate
of Heaven

The Blessed Virgin Mary is the gate of Heaven,
the portal of Paradise.
She is the way that leads to Life,
the path leading straight to eternal life.

Amadeus of Lausanne

The angels in Heaven rejoiced again! They sang, clapped their wings, and welcomed their Queen. Mary, having finished her life on earth, went up to Heaven, in body and soul. She is close to her Son, and she reigns with him forever.

By her Assumption, Mary prepared the way for us. She goes before us into Paradise. We too will live in Heaven, body and soul. That is the hope of Christians.

When I am dying, Mary will be close to me, ready to take me to Heaven with her.

Will I trust her completely?

Lord Jesus,
    through your mother Mary,
    you came to our world.
    Through you, she entered
    into the glory of Heaven.
    Give me your Spirit
    so that all my life
    I too can prepare
    to live forever
    in the joy of Heaven.

Mary, our Queen

A great sign appeared in heaven: a woman clothed with the sun, with the moon under her feet, and on her head a crown of twelve stars.

Revelation 12:1

Jesus is the King of the universe. He makes Mary, his mother, Queen of Heaven and earth. She holds the place of honour.

Her crown is the sign of her power. Mary is stronger than evil. She is the greatest of all God's creatures.

Did the angels really crown her with roses up there in Heaven? Did they use gold and precious stones? Or did they choose the most beautiful stars in the whole universe?

I want to make Mary the Queen of my heart. I'd like to be able to say to her, like Saint Louis-Marie Grignion de Montfort, "I am entirely yours, O Virgin Mary, and all that I have belongs to you."

I choose you today,
O Mary, in the presence
of all the heavenly choir,
as my mother and my Queen.

I consecrate to you
my body and my soul.

You may dispose of me
and of everything that belongs to me
without exception, however you like,
for the greater glory of God,
in time and in eternity.

(St Louis-Marie Grignion de Montfort)

Our Lady
of Prayer

*Mary kept all these things,
pondering them in her heart.*

Luke 2:19

Mary thought carefully about every event. Every important word, was engraved on her motherly heart. She remembered them, meditated on them, and prayed to know what God wanted to tell her. Mary was attentive: she wanted to do God's will, she wanted to serve him in everything. Mary teaches us to pray. She contemplates and listens. She shows us that praying is first of all watching how Jesus lives, and listening to his word.

To pray, we don't need to talk a lot. What we need to do is listen. Perhaps that's why when God made us, he gave us only one mouth, but two big ears!

O Mary, my mother,
so holy and so good!
Make me understand
the great value of the silence
in which I can hear God!
Teach me to keep quiet and listen to him.
Help me to make that into
a perfect prayer,
in faith, trust and love.

(From a prayer by Marthe Robin)

Our Lady
of the Rosary

The Rosary is my favourite prayer. A marvellous prayer! Marvellous in its simplicity and its depth.

John Paul II

The rosary is a very ancient and very simple prayer that the Church offers you so that you can come to love Jesus more and more, thanks to Mary. It's a bit like a chain – but not a chain for prisoners! It is a very light chain that links us to Heaven.

Each Hail Mary is like a rose that you offer to Mary. That's why this prayer is called the "rosary", because the word originally meant a rose-garden.

How do we pray the rosary? It's very simple. All we have to do is say five decades of the rosary while thinking about the life of Jesus.

Learn to pray the Rosary

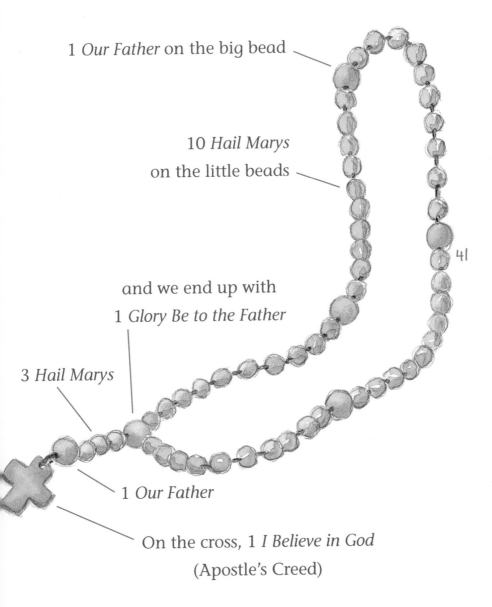

1 *Our Father* on the big bead

10 *Hail Marys*
on the little beads

and we end up with
1 *Glory Be to the Father*

3 *Hail Marys*

1 *Our Father*

On the cross, 1 *I Believe in God*
(Apostle's Creed)

41

Our Lady
of the Smile

*What penetrated to the depth of my soul
was our Lady's wonderful smile.*

St Thérèse of Lisieux

Saint Thérèse was ten years old when she became gravely ill and her family was very worried. They all prayed very hard to our Blessed Lady for her. One day, Thérèse saw the statue of Mary smiling at her. She got better in the next few hours. Our Lady's smile had brought her back to life.
In Mary's smile we can see all her love. Like Thérèse, let's allow ourselves to be cured by our mother's tender smile.

Even if I don't see the little statue in my prayer-corner smiling at me, I know it's true: Mary is there, close to me. She lights up my life with her motherly smile.

You are the safe port
for all shipwrecked sailors.
You are the mother of all orphans.
You are the hand
that breaks the chains.
You are the joy of the sick.
You are the smile returning to sad faces.
You are the sun of mankind,
O Mary, always.

(St Ephraim)

Our Lady of Mercy

I am all merciful.

Words of Mary to Estelle at Pellevoisin, 1856

Mary never abandons us. Whatever the situation, she comes to our help. She is the refuge of sinners: she welcomes us all under the great mantle of her love and mercy. She lets herself be touched by our trustful prayers.

Mary shows us how ugly our sins make us. She invites us to change our hearts so that we can receive God's love.

He is ready to forgive us for all our sins – his mercy is without end.

I can trust Mary: she prays to Jesus for me, and she teaches me to remain in his love. Holding tightly onto her hand, I'm not afraid of anything!

Remember,
O most loving Virgin Mary,
that never was it known
that anyone who fled
to your protection, implored your help,
or sought your intercession,
was left unaided.

Inspired by this confidence, I fly to you,
O Virgin of virgins, my Mother.
To you I come, before you I stand
sinful and sorrowful.

O Mother of the word Incarnate,
do not despise my petition,
but in your mercy hear and answer me.
Amen.

(St Bernard)

Mary
Mother of God

The Word became flesh and dwelt among us.

John 1:14

What great rejoicing there was in Ephesus one fine day in the year 431. All the Christians were singing and dancing in the streets, with immense joy, because the Bishops in council had just proclaimed Mary as "Theotokos". That's a Greek word that means "Mother of God". This is the greatest and most beautiful thing that can possibly be said about Mary. What could be more extraordinary than being called "Mother of God"? What an honour!

Mary is the Mother of Christ, true man. She brought him up, she formed his human heart.

Mary is the Mother of Christ, true God. She learnt from him who God is, and the greatness of God's love for all men.

How great and powerful Mary is! And yet the Mother of God is also my own mother, and I'm so little!

Hail Mary,
full of grace,
the Lord is with thee.
Blessed art thou amongst women,
and blessed is the fruit
of thy womb, Jesus.

Holy Mary, Mother of God,
pray for us sinners now
and at the hour of our death.
Amen.

CTS Children's Books

The Beautiful Story of Jesus, *by Maïte Roche*
(ISBN 978 1 86082 492 0 CTS Code CH 13)

Benedict & Chico, *by Jeanne Perego*
(ISBN 978 1 86082 493 7 CTS Code CH 12)

The Bible for little children, *by Maïte Roche*
(ISBN 978 1 86082 399 2 CTS Code CH 2)

Faith for Children, *by Christine Pedotti*
(ISBN 978 1 86082 447 0 CTS Code CH 9)

First prayers for little children, *by Maïte Roche*
(ISBN 978 1 86082 443 2 CTS Code CH 5)

The Gospel for little children, *by Maïte Roche*
(ISBN 978 1 86082 400 5 CTS Code CH 1)

The most beautiful Christmas Story, *by Maïte Roche*
(ISBN 978 1 86082 446 3 CTS Code CH 8)

Prayers around the Crib, *by Juliette Levivier*
(ISBN 978 1 86082 445 6 CTS Code CH 7)

Praying at Mass, *by Juliette Levivier*
(ISBN 978 1 86082 491 3 CTS Code CH 11)

Praying with Mary, *by Juliette Levivier*
(ISBN 978 1 86082 536 1 CTS Code CH 14)

Praying with the Holy Spirit, *by Juliette Levivier*
(ISBN 978 1 86082 537 8 CTS Code CH 15)

Praying with the first Chritians, *by Juliette Levivier*
(ISBN 978 1 86082 490 6 CTS Code CH 10)

Praying with the Friends of Jesus, *by Juliette Levivier*
(ISBN 978 1 86082 444 9 CTS Code CH 6)

The Rosary, *by Juliette Levivier*
(ISBN 978 1 86082 397 8 CTS Code CH 3)

The Way of the Cross, *by Juliette Levivier*
(ISBN 1 86082 398 X CTS Code CH 4)

Praying with the Holy Spirit: Published 2008 by The Incorporated Catholic Truth Society, 40-46 Harleyford Road, London SE11 5AY. Tel: 020 7640 0042; Fax: 020 7640 0046; www.cts-online.org.uk. Copyright © 2008 The Incorporated Catholic Truth Society in this English-language edition. Translated from the French edition by Geraldine Kay.

ISBN: 978 1 86082 537 8   CTS Code CH 15

Prier l'Esprit Saint by Juliette Levivier, illustrations by Anne Gravier, published 2008 by Edifa-Mame, 15-27 rue Moussorgski, 75018 Paris; ISBN Edifa 978-2-9163-5032-5; ISBN Mame 978-2-7289-1273-5. Copyright © Edifa Mame 2008.